ALL RI

M000223548

**"Produced by special arrangement with
Original Works Publishing."**
www.originalworksonline.com

Cover art by Paul Thureen—paulthureen@yahoo.com

Commencement
© 2010, Clay McLeod Chapman
Trade Edition, 2013
Printed in U.S.A.
ISBN 978-1-934962-65-7

Also Available From
Original Works Publishing

EIGHT
by Ella Hickson
Genre: Drama
Cast Size of 8

EIGHT swept the board at the biggest arts festival in the world, the Edinburgh Festival, in 2008. An underground hit propagated by sensational word-of-mouth, it went on to win a coveted Scotsman Fringe First Award, the NSDF Emerging Artists Award and the Carol Tambor 'Best of Edinburgh' Award, awarded to only one show across the thousands of productions at the festival.

Introducing eight beguiling oddballs, struggling to define what it is to be normal amidst the dissolution of social, moral, sexual and cultural boundaries in The Naughties. From high-class hookers to those who make friends in morgues, to single mothers and bereaved gallery owners, Eight gives all of these otherwise neglected characters center-stage, including the moving, politically punchy portrait of a man who has lost everything except his memories of the 7/7 London bombings (*"One of the finest pieces of writing I've yet heard about the aftermath of that terrible day"* – Joyce McMillan, The Scotsman).

Radio Star
by Tanya O'Debra
Genre: Comedy
1 Female

Synopsis: *Radio Star* is a 1940's radio detective spoof. In *The Case of the Long Distance Lover*, Nick McKitrick; Private Dick, is hired by femme fatale Fanny LaRue to find her husband's killer. The plot is a standard mystery, but Radio Star's contemporary sense of humor sets it apart from the pack. A laugh out loud radio romp, easily produced with one actress or a larger cast.

Michelle
Hill

commencement

written by
Clay McLeod Chapman

Commencement was originally commissioned in 2009 by Company of Fools (Denise Simone and John Glenn, Core Company Artists) in Hailey, Idaho.

Special thanks to Denise Simone and John Glenn at Company of Fools, Erez Ziv and Heidi Grumelot at Horse Trade, Melissa Rindell, Emily Owens, Shelley Miles, Barbara Clark at The Barbara Clark Agency and Indrani Sen.

<u>Cast breakdown:</u>

One performer, female – three characters

Part I – *staph infection:* Sarah Havermeyer (age 41)

Part II – *early release:* Julie Keady (age 17)

Part III – *keynote speaker:* Mary Keady (age 42)

for Hanna Cheek

AUTHOR'S NOTE:

Though there are three female characters in *Commencement*, it is strongly encouraged that all be played by the same performer. The desired effect is to present that alchemical moment within the third segment (*keynote speaker*) where each woman's story finally interconnects during the delivery of Julie Keady's graduation speech. This intersection is performative – where our actress must shift from one character to the next with a certain fluidity, gradually transitioning from Sarah Havermeyer reading Julie's speech to Julie herself. Though it is Sarah who is reading the speech – for Mary Keady, Sarah's voice slips away and is replaced by Julie's, hearing her daughter through her own words. In this respect, Julie is able to deliver her speech as if it were her graduation day.

part one: *staph infection*

Sarah Havermeyer, *forty-one*

They gave me my own waiting room. Hid me in the pediatric wing, far away from the other families. It's much quieter at this end of the hospital. Less hectic here. Less parents, less press. Spent the last hour simply listening to the hum of fluorescents over my head.

Went over to the window on a whim once, lured in by the camera flashes. The parking lot's all gone now. It's suddenly engulfed in a forest of transmission antennas, budding up from the roofs of these news vans. The network call letters look like initials of young couples carved into the bark of each tree. *KBCW-TV plus WGBO-4. WDBJ-7 hearts WSLS-10 4-eva...*

When Mitchell was much younger, he and handful of kids from the neighborhood all went out into the woods behind our houses to play a game of hide-and-seek. When it was Mitchell's turn to be *it*, he leaned his head against his own tree just as everyone else had before him. Closed his eyes and counted to a hundred.

By the time he turned back around, he found himself facing the woods all alone. *Ready or not, here I come* – echoing through the trees. But what Mitchell didn't realize – and why would he, really – was that everybody else had already run home by then. Didn't stop him from playing, though. Peeking behind each tree. Searching for his friends.

An hour went by before I was on the phone with the neighbors, asking if they knew where Mitchell was. But none of their kids would say, shrugging their shoulders. When there weren't any parents left to call, I took to the woods myself. Flashlight in hand. Finally found him leaning against a tree, huddled into himself. *Shivering.* Poor thing caught pneumonia that night. Had to take him to the hospital, waiting in this same room.

Want to tell me what happened?

No.

We can keep it between you and me, if you'd like. Promise I won't tell.

I don't want to talk about it.

There are never any magazines here. Nothing but coloring books flung across the floor. Crayons scattered all around, like shell casings discharged from a rifle. Every color of the rainbow falling to the floor, round after round after round...

Not that I feel like reading right now. Simply had that reflex to flip through something. Get my mind off things. Picked up a coloring book without even realizing what it was at first, skimming the pictures just to pass the time. Glancing at all the empty animals, empty cartoon characters. Page after page. Their blank bodies filled in with scribbles, crayon spread everywhere. No consideration for coloring in the lines, whatsoever. You'd think they'd all been shot, every animal hemorrhaging Crayola across the page. Their splatter pattern in *Razzle Dazzle Rose* or *Tickle Me Pink*.

The amount of times I've sat here over the years, waiting amongst all the other mothers – I've lost count by now. They blend together after a while. All the check-ups. The mumps. Flu shots. Chicken pox. Not to mention ear infections. A tonsillectomy. A sprained wrist. The list just goes on and on...

It's a wonder my son even reached high school.

How any of our children made it this far.

Not that the news is saying anything. Not until the police notify the next of kin. The reporters have been recycling the same information for hours now, the live coverage sounding stale already.

No names yet. Just numbers.

Last time I had to wait this long, it was because Mitchell had swallowed something he shouldn't have. *Marbles*. Started complaining about his tummy aching at the dinner table, refusing to finish his macaroni – so the very next day, I brought him in for an X-ray. And sure enough, there they were – a constellation of bright white contrasting against that ghastly black of his stomach. The negative image of a half dozen glass pellets settled into his belly. A grape cluster tethered together in pale veins.

Benjamin Pendleton had put him up to it. Said he'd be his *best friend* if he swallowed the whole set, all ten marbles. And to think that Mitchell had almost made it, more than halfway there – determined to earn

Benjamin Pendleton's approval, to win this position as his pal, *bestest friends*, only giving up once his throat constricted itself, his own esophagus refusing to swallow anymore, no matter how hard he tried, no matter how hard he forced himself to eat one more, *just one more*, begging with his own throat to let him ingest just one last marble before stumbling back home, sick to his stomach.

To *prove* his worth. As a *friend* to Benjamin.

Want to tell me who put you up to this?

No.

Mitchell – you're only hurting yourself by not saying anything.

I don't want to talk about it.

The police have been ushering all the parents in through the rear entrance of the hospital, away from the camera crews. The second I saw Wendy Pendleton in the hallway, barely able to even stand on her own two feet – I knew why she was here. Recognized her right away, even though we hadn't spoken to each other in ages. Not since our sons were in the third grade together.

12

Her eyes had glazed over. Nothing but a pair of marbles settled into each socket, flickering under the fluorescents. Felt like I was staring at a teddy bear. Not some mother who'd just identified her son.

They've placed a police officer right outside my door. *For my protection,* they say. They're worried some wandering father might find me here, hiding amongst the stuffed animals. The jigsaw puzzles. The coloring books with the mottled corners, their pages sticking together from all the constant gnawing. Seems as if children chose to chew through these books rather than read them. The edges are still wet, even after office hours have come and gone for the day. The pulp rubs right off between my fingers. I'm thinking of the poor puzzle with its missing pieces, all of them dissolving inside some sick kid's stomach. Nurses have to sanitize these toys at the end of every day, spraying them down with disinfectant. They have to kill off the bacteria before the following morning – before it starts up all over again. One child will pass along their germs to whoever puts the same stuffed animal's filthy limb into their mouth next. They'll end up catching something completely different than whatever it was they walked in here with.

Seems fitting to be sitting here then. Almost like old times. Wouldn't be so surprised if a nurse were to walk in any minute now, calling out Mitchell's name – *The doctor will see you now.*

But none of the nurses will even come near me now. Won't look me in the eye. Passing them all in the hallway, they'd simply bow their heads. Focus on the linoleum rather than face me. As if they were afraid? *Of me?*

The press is about to take my boy away from me. This is my last chance to have him all to myself, the way I want to remember him – before I have to give him up. Let him go.

I'm imagining some reporter sifting through the yearbook, flipping from page to page just to find his photograph. Before long, Mitchell's face will be broadcast all over the news – which is unfortunate, since he never took his class pictures seriously. He'd never tell me what day they were being taken, just so I couldn't force him to dress up. Look nice for his picture. By the time I'd find out, it was always too late. They would've already snapped off the shot. If I ever wanted to order any photos for the rest of the family, I'd have to buy these wallet-sized prints of him in one of his ratty t-shirts. His hair all tussled. Refusing to smile for the camera.

Can't even bring myself to look at his yearbook now. Seeing him there, surrounded by the rest. Their faces clumped together, grinning all around him.

Nothing but an obituary now – the whole year-book. This grim assembly of smiles.

The world will weep for the children of Midlothian High – but no one will weep for mine. I'll have to cry for my child alone. You won't find his name amongst the others. He's been omitted from the list of victims. Not that he was ever invited into their club anyways. Mitchell was never asked to play with the rest. They'll say it was my son who took their children away – but what none of these parents are willing to admit is that their sons and daughters took my child away from me long before today. Mitchell had the bruises to prove it. Half of our trips to the hospital were for fractures that magically happened on their own. Sprained wrists that mysteriously appeared out of nowhere, no explanation whatsoever. Black eyes that looked like black holes, swallowing up my son, the distance deepening within his gaze.

Every time, *every time* I've had to sit here in this room, I've lost a little bit more of my son. It was only a matter of time before there was nothing left of him to take back home.

Can we talk?

...Why?

Want to tell me what's been on your mind lately?

No.

Anything happening at school?

No.

What about —

Mom.

Can't we just chat? Just for a minute?

There's nothing to talk about.

There's plenty.

Just let it go, mom.

Please, honey...

I said no. Just drop it, alright?

All I want is to sit with the rest of the parents. I want to wait amongst the other mothers. To mourn with them. I've lost my child, too. Why can't I sit with them?

We deserve to wait together.

Found a stray puzzle piece at my feet, softened with some child's saliva. There's no telling what the picture's of. Has a fleshy complexion. Even feels like flesh, the cardboard all soaked in spit. Its interlocking tabs are so flimsy, they'll flap back and forth whenever I rub my fingers over them.

Came across another piece tucked just behind the leg of my chair. Same color, same wet texture. The two pieces fit together perfectly.

Suddenly the picture's coming into view. Here's a piece of his cheek. A tooth. A shard of his skull, a clump of his hair matted down in blood. Fragments of his face, the skin still adhered to the bone.

I'm picking up what's left of him off the floor. The hundreds of tessellating flecks of flesh and bone, blown off at close range. Passing the time working on this jigsaw puzzle of my son's face, just to get one last look at him.

High muzzle velocity. When Mitchell was done, he slipped the gun over his tongue. The blast reached through the roof of his mouth. Ruptured all the soft tissue before bursting through the back of his skull, sending puzzle pieces all over the classroom wall.

Kids will put anything into their mouths.

part two: *early release*

Julie Keady, *seventeen*

Give me a name. Any name. Pick any student from this school and I bet you I can list off all the books they've ever checked out without even needing to use the computer.

It's a talent I have. Got a lot of time on my hands here. Besides – it's more fun to flip to the back of the book, to the index card holstered along the cover. All the students who've ever checked it out are right there – a winding column of names in different colored inks, different handwriting. Dates winding backwards. Some so far back, well before I had ever set foot into this school – the names don't even sound real anymore.

Like ghosts.

Mitchell's name pops up in a lot of library books. More than most students here. Sometimes his name is the only one listed, written five times on top of each other. Ten times. Filling up the whole card. *Do Androids Dream of Electric Sheep?* October 15th to November 2nd.

Slaughterhouse-Five. January 10th to the 23rd. *A Clockwork Orange.* February 13th to March 6th.

One Flew Over The Cuckoos Nest. Page 86. In the margins, in different colors of ink, you can read:

So – what'd you think?

What?

The book. Did you like it?

The movie was better.

You should totally check out Animal Farm. It's about communism – but with pigs.

I started eating lunch in the library as early as my freshman year. Spent my study halls there already, shelving books for extra credit. I'd always been a bookworm at heart, no matter what my friends said. They'd tease me about it all the time, but I was itching for Ivy League and needed my transcripts to prove it.

One of my jobs here was to flip through the books. Find the vandalism. White-Out the dirty doodles. Erase all the explicit scribbles. That sort of thing.

Mitchell would take notes. He circled words. Phrases were underlined. Particular passages were boxed in with pencil. Felt guilty for having to rub out his thoughts. I'd read over all his annotations before erasing them, seeing if I could figure out what he thought about the book. Whether or not he liked it.

Nobody else checked out the books he did. Not in a long time.

Breakfast of Champions. Page 45. In the margins, in different handwriting, you can read:

Since you've already departed from the required reading list, you should totally read Naked Lunch next.

What's that?

William S. Burroughs. We're not allowed to carry it here – but I've got a copy at home, if you're interested. I could let you borrow it. I'll leave it on the third bookshelf, second aisle. Between Whitman and Wordsworth.

Whatever.

Students will say they each had a moment. An encounter with Mitchell that they never mentioned before. Never brought up. Not until now, when everyone's looking. At the time, they'll say, it didn't seem like such a big deal. But now – now – if they'd only told a teacher, maybe, just maybe, things would be different today. Maybe they could've stopped this all from happening. They want to say they saw the warning signs. They want to lay claim to've known all along. Truth is – none of them ever cared. Mitchell Havermeyer was a social ghost, haunting the hallways of this school long before he shot himself. Students will never let him go. He's all ours now. Our own boogeyman mascot.

Mitchell would sit by himself in the library, always with some book open before him. His mom still packed his lunch. Always the same sandwich – PB/J. A Granny Smith and a Zip-Lock full of Oreos. Four Oreos. A can of soda with a napkin wrapped around it, soaking up the condensation so that it clung to the can. And on the napkin – a note from his mom, written in magic marker. The words were all blurred, the letters loosened by the wetness, ink bleeding into the napkin.

Brave New World. Page 132. In the margins, half in cursive, the other half in print, you can read:

Have you read Lord of the Flies yet? Think you'd like it.

How do you know? You don't know anything about me.

This was totally against library policy, I know. The librarians would've kicked me out if I'd gotten caught. But I had an idea. Since Mitchell checked out the same books more than once, as soon as he'd return them and I'd have to attend to my requisite scribble rinsing – I'd find his notes in the margins and try responding with some of my own. *Pen-pals.* It'd be fun. It'd all be there, everything we ever wrote – our correspondence tucked away in the pages, where no one would find us. No one would ever know.

Establishing contact had to begin broad. Had to cast a wide net, responding to four or five of his favorites. It was impossible to tell which book he'd choose to check out next. I had to look at his patterns, trying to determine what he'd want to read all over again.

1984 or *The Dharma Bums. Catcher in the Rye* or *I Am Legend.*

First contact was in *On the Road*, page 33: *What's up?*

Simple. Straightforward. Nothing too complicated. Wrote it right below a bunch of his notes before slipping the books back on the shelves. Didn't sign my name or anything, keeping it anonymous.

Two weeks later, his response: *Who's this?*

I wrote back: *Did you know Kerouac wrote this book on an endless sheet of paper?*

Two weeks later: *So what?*

I wrote back: *He didn't want to waste time switching out sheets, so he fed a whole roll into his typewriter. That way he could just keep writing and writing and never stop. Pretty cool, huh?*

Two weeks later: *Sort of.*

A chain of exchanges started to stretch down the margins, each link in different ink. Took a month to fill up a single page – but it was working. We were talking. Sort of talking.

In *Neuromancer* I wrote: *Did you know William Gibson came up with the internet before anyone else had even thought of it?*

Two weeks later: *Really?*

I wrote: *Cyberspace was totally his idea.*

Two weeks later: *That's pretty cool.*

I could pop up in any book at any time. He'd never see me coming – but once I was there, we'd deface the pages together, filling up the margins for entire chapters. Whenever we would've exhausted the blank boundaries of one book, we'd move on to another.

See you in Fear and Loathing in Las Vegas, page 86.

Catch you in The Plague, chapter three.

Find me in Nova Express, page 23.

We would run out of books at the rate we were writing now, burning through the whole library before the end of the school year.

Where do we go from here?

How about a bigger book? Like Dostoevsky or something? That way we'll have some space...

Okay.

Crime and Punishment, page 42.

We never said anything to each other outside of our correspondence. Passing him in the halls, I acted as if I didn't know. Nobody did. None of my friends, nobody. Our lives outside of our messages didn't matter. It didn't matter who we were here – who was popular and who wasn't. We had created a space completely independent of high school politics. In these books, we were free to be whoever who we really were. Nothing else mattered.

A Confederacy of Dunces. Page 312. In the margins, in interlacing handwriting, weaving together like a braid of hair, you can read:

Who are you?

Don't you know? A friend.

What makes you think I'm your friend?

Because only ghosts can see other ghosts.

I wanted him to know that I saw him. That no matter how shitty the kids at this school treated him, he wasn't alone.

We wrote each other for all the fall, through the whole winter. We'd kept our correspondence secret for nearly the whole school year. I was asked to give a speech for our graduation. Still shelved books for extra credit during study hall, but suddenly I was spending less time in the library – using my lunchperiod to work on what I was going to say to the rest of the school. Everyone kept asking me – *What're you going to write? What're you going to write?* Over and over again, like a broken record.

Everybody but Mitchell.

He was supposed to return a book to the library the day of the shooting. When study hall came and went and he hadn't brought it back, I wondered where he could be. Usually he returned his books on time. He'd had the book out for the full two weeks. It'd be overdue by the end of school. He'd be fined ten cents for each day he didn't bring the book back to me.

I'd been sitting in history, working on my graduation speech when I heard a pop outside. We all heard it; the whole class. Could've been band practice. The drum corps must've been rehearsing in the hallway, the rapid fire of a snare rattling through the rest of the school. But the rhythm felt awkward. The tempo was off. There was a quick succession of bursts – then nothing. Again – one beat, two. Silence.

Then we heard screaming.

Mitchell walked right into room 202. This wasn't his class. For a second, I thought he must've found out that I was his pen-pal – barging in like he'd been looking for me all day, wanting to let me know he'd finally figured it out.

Kim Young-Lee had been sitting beside me. I watched her flop over onto her desk, as if she'd fallen asleep all of a sudden. Carl Santoro was sitting on the other side. His body slithered out from his desk, slumping to the floor. Jamie Temple used to sit with me on the school bus when we were in kindergarten – and here he was, one row back, right behind me, taking a bullet directly into his chest.

There was a pop. Then another. Felt this pressure against my chest.

I looked up at Mitchell and realized he didn't recognize me.

The shelves have felt emptier since the shooting. The tally is two dozen books by my count – all of them long overdue. The students who checked them out are all dead now.

How's the library supposed to get those books back?

Third aisle. Second shelf from the top. Fifteen books in. Between Emily Bronte and William Cullen Bryant. You'll find the last book Mitchell ever checked out. His last act as a student here at Midlothian High School was to return his library book. It's been reshelved, back on the stacks. No one's checked it out since. No one probably ever will again.

Robert Browning. *The Pied Piper of Hamelin*. The title circled. It's his pen. Same ink. Particular passages underlined. Complete stanzas cordoned off.

Flip to page 18. In the margin, in Mitchell's handwriting, you can read Mitchell's last correspondence:

Where'd you go?

He never realized I was his pen-pal. Now he'll never know. No one will.

This is where I live now. This is my home.

part three: *keynote speaker*

Mary Keady, *forty-two*

Julie was supposed to deliver this year's commencement speech. She'd agonized over it for weeks. Fretted over every sentence, wanting each word to be perfect. I'd peek my head into her room whenever I'd see her lights still on late at night, finding her fast asleep at her desk. Her cheek resting on what she'd written thus far. Took every bit of willpower I could muster not to read it, peering over her shoulder.

You're gonna have to wait until graduation, mom, she'd say, catching me red-handed. *You'll hear it along with everybody else.*

Julie always sat in the front of her class, no matter what the subject. Always tried to be as close to the chalkboard as humanly possible. Never wanted another student's head blocking her view.

She took three bullets – all by herself. The entrance wounds lined up along her chest, like a row of red ribbons, the rosettes bursting through her shirt, as if she'd fallen short from taking home first prize at this year's science fair: *second place second place second place…*

Graduation was sparse this year. Less in attendance, less parents. Half the families who'd lost their children didn't even show. The Pendletons. The O'Rourkes. The Connors.

I went. My husband had been against going – but I made him attend anyways. I wanted to hear this year's keynote speaker. I wanted someone to make sense of what had happened – and who better, really? I wanted to hear what their advice would be for the future. What words of wisdom they'd dole out to the students who survived.

Aim high. Achieve your dreams. Don't give up.

They got our Governor to step in at the last minute. To ease our school's collective pain. He spoke of healing. He spoke of forgiveness. But he didn't speak to me.

Brought along my camera. Didn't seem right to go

to graduation without it. I listened as each student was called up, one at a time. Their names echoed throughout the auditorium, the loudspeakers making them sound hollow. When they finally reached the K's, I pulled out my camera, ready to snap off a shot, listening to the assistant principal run through Kagan, Kagebeck, Kahn.

Julie Keady. She'll rise up from the mass of gowns and tassels, taking the stage.

Julie Keady. She'll step up to the principal and shake his hand, receiving her diploma with the other.

Julie Keady. She'll turn towards the audience, facing every parent sitting in that auditorium. Waving her certificate in the air. And I will be right there, clicking off the picture. Saving that moment forever.

Julie...

They skipped over her name. Hopped right onto Anne Kellaway and just kept on going. Lancaster. Lassiter. Lee. I listened to her slip farther and farther away from me. Manuella. Matthews. Ming. Why wouldn't they let her graduate?

I'd been weeding our garden when the phone rang. I figured the answering machine would pick it up, so I didn't budge. Just kept on digging. But as soon as the machine would click on, the person on the other end would hang up and call back. Had to've been a salesman soliciting for something. *Are you happy with your current phone service provider?* Who else would keep calling like that? Over and over again. You'd think they'd leave a message if it was so important. Here I am – on my hands and knees. All covered in dirt. Certainly wasn't about to track mud all over the kitchen floor just to answer the phone.

That's why I was the last parent to the hospital. Bill had beaten me to it. The police had called him from work. He'd already identified Julie's body by the time I got there, sitting amongst all the other parents in the waiting room. No need to identify her again.

But the police weren't going to let me see. They told me I was too late. If I wanted to see Julie for myself, I'd have to wait.

Wait for what? I asked. *What else is there?*

We buried her the day after graduation. More parents showed up to the memorial service than our own kids' commencement, forced to swap ceremonies at the last moment. For those families that had lost their children – rather than watch them graduate, we all attended each other's funerals. I saw the Pendletons. The O'Rourkes. The Connors.

No Sarah Havermeyer. Her son wasn't amongst ours. Mitchell's yearbook picture wasn't one of the dozen framed photographs wrapped in their own floral wreath, standing upright at the front for all to see. I turned around at one point during the service, sifting through all the students and teachers. Just to see if I could find her. See if she'd show up. Pay her respects.

Julie's principal took to the podium, directly addressing all the parents. He spoke to us of healing. He spoke of forgiveness. But he didn't speak to me.

The police returned Julie's backpack after they'd rummaged through it. Her commencement speech had been inside, tucked into her French textbook. Couldn't bring myself to read it – when only a few days before, there was nothing in this world that I wanted to do more. *Nothing in this world.* I tried. Several times, I held the paper up to my face, making it as far as the first sentence before the back of my throat would begin to burn.

Her words deserved to be heard. They needed to be read out loud. Because letters of acceptance keep coming in, even now. All the scholarship offers. The study guides. Because colleges keep sending Julie housing surveys to figure out which dorm she'll be living in next year.

Because she never got to read it herself. Because she never got to stand up at that podium and share her words with the rest of her friends, ushering the graduating class into the real world.

Because I was robbed of watching her walk.

Because we deserved commencement.

Because I'm fed up with the empty rhetoric. All these speeches, these promises of pushing on.

Because of her son. *Because of her son.*

My daughter finally graduated today. Sarah Havermeyer was the keynote speaker.

She didn't answer the door right away. I could sense her on the other side the door, leaning into the peephole. There was no need to ring the bell again but I went ahead and did it anyway, acting as if I didn't realize she was standing there, staring back at me.

Mary? She kept the chain-lock between us.

Sarah... Can we talk?

I don't know, Mary. My lawyer said I shouldn't...

Please – just let me in.

The ceremony was simple. Just the two of us, together. Alone in her house. In her living room. The front door shut, sealing us inside. The ticking of a clock from another room. Pictures of him, of Mitchell as a kid, nothing but a little boy, framed on the wall. Watching over us. And Julie's speech – that single sheet of notebook paper, folded and refolded over a dozen different times.

We called out their names. We called up the graduating class. Sean Connor. Paul Hastings. Kim Young-Lee. Robert Marasco. Benjamin Pendleton. Tammy O'Rourke. Carl Santoro. Jamie Temple. Julie

Keady. We watched them rise up from the mass of gowns. Their tassels continuing to grow. God help me – I saw worms. Like a million wriggling diplomas – I couldn't stop myself from seeing them. Flinging their hats high, the air above our heads eclipsed in graduation caps – their edges as sharp as shovel blades, breaking open the earth and burying their bodies.

Read it.

Please, Mary... Please don't make me do this.

Read the speech. Now.

Sarah brought the paper up to her face, sobbing. The page was only inches away from her mouth, getting wet. The words were distorting, unleashing their ink.

What is graduation? Some say it's the end of the best years of our lives. Now that we're about to enter into the real world – there's one big question that's lingering within all of our minds: What happens next?

Hearing her speech, quivering out from Sarah Havermeyer's mouth – all I could do was close my eyes and listen. Let the words take me away.

And for a moment, for just a brief moment – I could hear her again. Her words had come alive.

My baby girl had finally graduated.

Most graduation speeches talk about how close we've become as a class. But ten years from now – we won't be chanting Go Trojans! or Senior Power! We'll be remembering the friendships we made, the relationships we shared.

For once – we all look the same. Blue gowns. Tassels on top of our hats. But even though we look alike in this very moment, it's our differences that make us who we are. I believe each one of us here has the potential to become something special. To become someone. To make something out of our lives and change the world as we know it.

So back to that big question: What happens next?

I say the answer is: Anything we want…

About The Author

Clay McLeod Chapman is the author of "rest area," a collection of short stories, and "miss corpus," a novel. "Miss corpus" was recognized in part of The New Yorker's "Reading Glasses" series in 2003.

Currently, he is writing a trilogy of children's novels titled "The Tribe"—book one, "Homeroom Headhunters," hits the shelves in 2013 on Hyperion books.

Recently, Chapman's story "the battle of belle isle" was featured in Akashic Books' regional-noir anthology "Richmond Noir." He was a contributing author on "The Rolling Darkness Revue," a roaming reading-series of horror writers created by Glen Hirshberg and Pete Atkins, culminating in the anthology At The Sign of the Snowman's Skull. He was a contributing author to One Ring Zero's "As Smart As We Are" album, featuring such writers as Paul Auster and Jonathan Lethem.will occasionally write from time to time for his geek-gods Marvel Comics and Fangoria Magazine.

Chapman's story "late bloomer" was adapted into film by director Craig Macneill. An official selection at the 2005 Sundance Film Festival, the short won the audience award for Best Short at the Lake Placid Film Festival and the Brown Jenkins Award at the 12th Annual H.P. Lovecraft Film Festival. Their most recent collaboration, "Henley," a short film based on the chapter "The Henley Road Motel" from his novel "miss corpus," was an official selection at the 2012 Sundance Film Festival. It was awarded Best Short Film at the 2011 Gen Art Film Festival and the 2011 Carmel Arts and Film Festival.

Upcoming films include a feature length version of "Henley," produced by The Woodshed (Elijah Wood, Daniel Noah, and Josh C. Waller) and Parent Company Films (Noah Greenberg) andsci-fried feature "White Space."

Chapman is the creator of the rigorous storytelling session The Pumpkin Pie Show. In its ten-plus years of existence, it has performed internationally at the Romanian Theatre Festival of Sibiu, the Edinburgh Fringe Festival, the New York International Fringe Festival, the Winnipeg Fringe Festival, the Edmonton Fringe Festival, the Minnesota Fringe Festival, the Dublin-based thisisnotashop art space, IGNITE Festival, the Women Center Stage Festival and the Impact Theatre Festival. The Pumpkin Pie Show continues to perform in New York City annually with long-time scene-stealer Hanna Cheek.

Chapman has written the book for the musical "Hostage Song" with music and lyrics by Obie-winner Kyle Jarrow. He also wrote the book for "SCKBSTD," a new musical with Grammy-winner

Bruce Hornsby. He is the author of such plays as "commencement," "teaser cow," "JULIAN," "bar flies," "lee's miserables," "No Exitway," "duct-tape to family-time," "drinking games," "redbird," "jewish mothers," "junta high," "nested doll," "the interstate and on," "the cardiac shadow" and "volume of smoke." Stage versions of his short stories "birdfeeder" and "undertow" were selected for publication in The Best American Short Plays: 2007-2008 and 2009-2010 anthologies.

Chapman was educated at the North Carolina School of the Arts for Drama, the Burren College of Art, and Sarah Lawrence College. He currently teaches writing at The Actors Studio MFA Program at Pace University.

claymcleodchapman.com

NOTES

20943795R10027

Made in the USA
San Bernardino, CA
30 April 2015